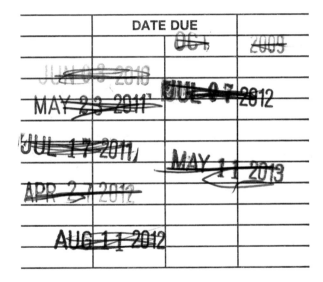

INSECTS

BIGGEST! LITTLEST!

Sandra Markle

Photographs by Dr. Simon Pollard

BOYDS MILLS PRESS

HONESDALE, PENNSYLVANIA

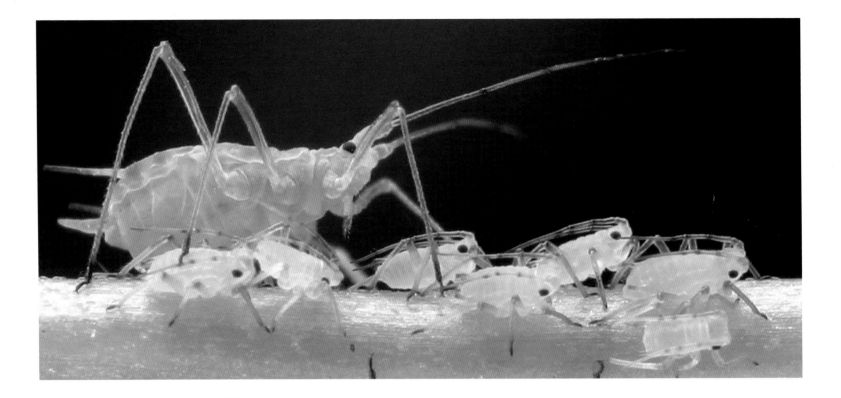

Some insects are little.

The bigger insect is an adult female Pea Aphid.

She's so little she could fit on the head of a pin.

The even littler aphids are her babies.

Some insects are big.

This one is a Giant Stick Insect that lives in Borneo.

Some are as much as 22 inches (56 centimeters) long.

It's one of the world's biggest kinds of insects.

Look at it next to this man's hand.

This Giant Stick Insect is a female.

Females grow to be even bigger than males.

No matter their size, big or little, adult insects have six legs and three main body parts: a head, a thorax, and an abdomen.

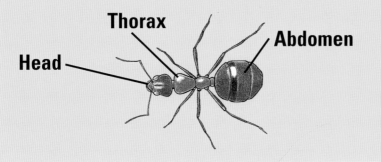

So why be big?

It helps insects like the Giant Stick Insect and this Weta (WET-uh) stay safe.

An adult female Weta is about 3½ inches (9 centimeters) long.

That makes a Weta too big a mouthful for most predators, animals that catch and eat other animals.

If the Weta is attacked, it throws up its spiny rear legs.

That keeps most hunters from getting close enough to bite.

Being big helps this female Praying Mantis catch big prey, like this spider.

Some kinds of Mantises grow to be as much as 6 inches (15.24 centimeters) long.

The females of most kinds of insects are bigger than the males.

They need to be bigger to hold all the eggs they produce.

Eating bigger prey gives them the energy they need to produce eggs.

This Raja Brooke Birdwing Butterfly is one of the biggest kinds of butterflies.

Spread out, its wings stretch nearly a foot (30 centimeters).

The Raja Brooke Birdwing Butterfly lives in Malaysia's tropical rain forests—a habitat full of colorful plants.

Scientists believe this butterfly's big wings may work like a colorful banner and help mates find each other.

So why be little?

Being little means this Western Pygmy Blue Butterfly is less likely to be seen by predators, like birds.

The Western Pygmy Blue Butterfly is one of the littlest kinds of butterflies.

Spread out, its wings are no more than 1/2 inch (about 12 millimeters) across.

That's about the size of an average adult human's littlest fingernail.

For the Minute Pirate Bug, being little means not competing for food.

Less than 1/8 inch (about 2 millimeters) long, this adult female eats tiny prey, like these Whitefly young, called larvae (LAR-vee).

Sometimes she eats even tinier insect eggs.

So the Minute Pirate Bug can live on prey too tiny for bigger insects to bother with.

Whitefly larvae

Some insects have big body parts that are important to how they live.

Butterflies and moths have a proboscis (pro-BAH-sis).

This straw-like mouthpart lets them reach inside flowers to drink nectar, a sweet liquid.

But a Hummingbird Hawkmoth's proboscis is extra-long.

It lets the moth reach inside tube-shaped flowers that are too long for other nectar sippers.

Weevils, like this Elephant Weevil, have a head shaped like a big snout.

Their jaws are at the tip.

That's perfect for boring into grapevines and branches of fruit trees.

They drill in to eat the plant material inside.

That food is too tough for most insects to reach.

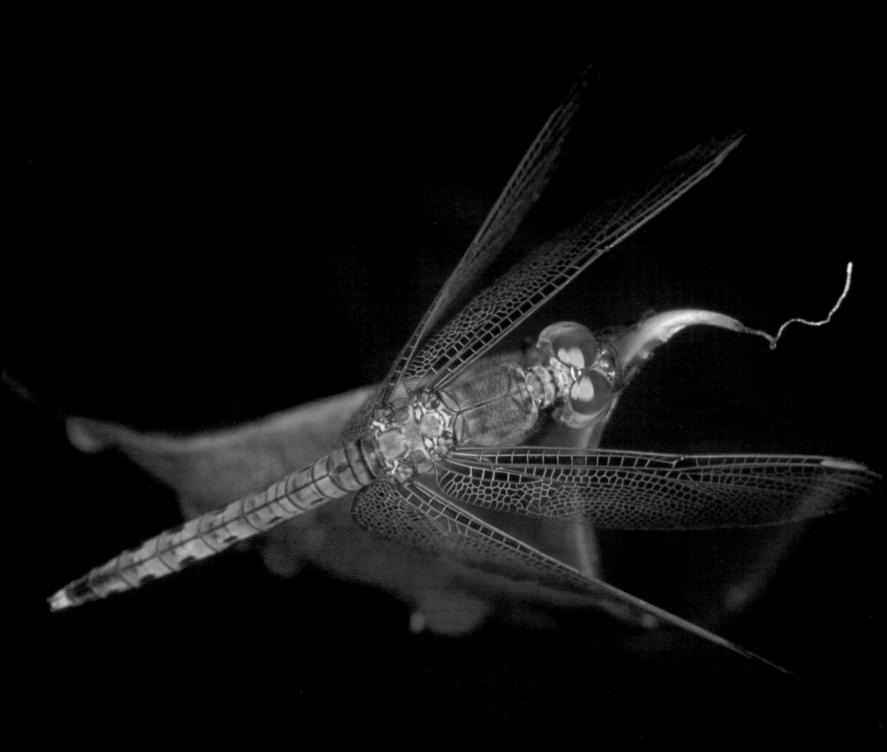

Dragonflies have great big eyes.

But each big eye is really lots of little eye units packed together.

The many eye units let the dragonfly look up, down, left, and right all at once.

This way, the dragonfly quickly spots its prey: mosquitoes, midges, flies, and other flying insects.

Then the dragonfly flaps its big wings and zips off to catch a meal in midair.

Dragonflies are the fastest insects. Scientists have recorded them flying as fast as 36 miles (almost 60 kilometers) per hour.

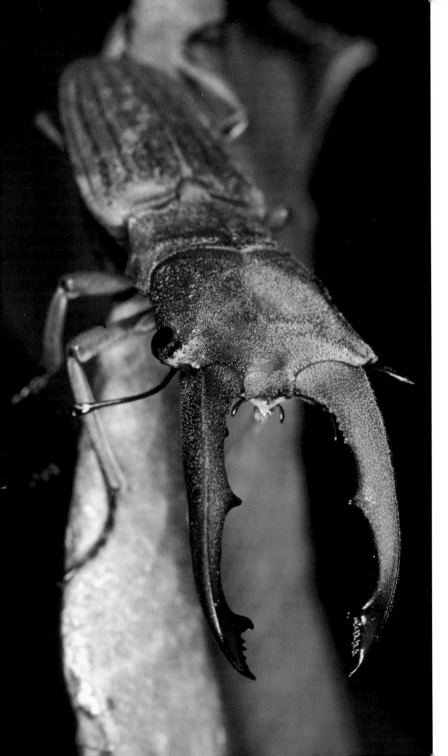

Male Stag Beetles have really big jaws.

Males may be as much as 3$\frac{1}{8}$ inches (8 centimeters) long.

Look how much of that length is big mouthparts.

Males use their jaws to fight other males for a chance to mate.

Female Stag Beetles have only average-sized jaws.

Eyestalk

Eyestalk

Male Stalk-Eyed Flies have really big eyestalks.

Rather than fighting for a mate, these males duel.

They face off and touch eyes.

The male with the longest eyestalks wins.

Female Stalk-Eyed Flies have much shorter eyestalks.

17

Some insects have little body parts that make a big difference.

The Toothbrush Caterpillar would just naturally be an easy meal for most predators.

But it has stiff bunches of little hairs on its back.

These hairs make it too prickly a mouthful for most hungry hunters.

Can you guess why it is called the Toothbrush Caterpillar?

This Geometer Moth Caterpillar shows another case of little parts that have a big effect.

The caterpillar would be soft and easy to munch.

But most predators don't even see it.

It is covered with little bumps.

The bumps help the caterpillar blend in with the twig it's on.

So the caterpillar only has to stay still to hide.

Some insects are little but part of a big group.

Working together lets these Carpenter Ants multiply their hunting power.

One ant stung the caterpillar.

It injected a little venom, which is a liquid poison.

But that was not enough to kill the caterpillar.

Then lots more ants attacked.

Soon the caterpillar was dead.

The ants will rip their prey apart and carry the food home to their nest.

Honeybees team up to drive enemies away from their hive.

They also work together to keep the hive from being too hot or too cold.

If the hive heats up, lots of bees fan their wings.

If the hive cools off, lots of bees shiver.

Each bee can give off only a tiny bit of heat.

But lots of bees shivering at once will do the trick.

Insects don't just get bigger to become adults.

They change.

Some insects, like these Paper Wasps, develop through four stages: egg, larva (LAR-vuh), pupa (PYU-puh), and adult.

A single adult female, the queen, lays the eggs, one in each of the cells in the paper nest.

Once the larvae hatch, other adults, the workers, take care of them.

The adults are big wasps, 2 inches (about 5 centimeters) long.

They catch insects to feed the larvae.

They also use their big stingers to protect the larvae from predators, like birds or snakes.

When a larva is ready for the pupa stage, the adults cover its cell with a paper cap.

Adult

Larvae

Pupae

Growing up in these four stages—egg, larva, pupa, and adult—is called complete metamorphosis (MEH-tuh-MOR-feh-sis). Metamorphosis means "change."

Now larval body parts break down, and adult body parts build up.

Finally, the pupa becomes an adult.

It chews open the paper cap and crawls out.

Other insects, like Praying Mantises, develop through three stages: egg, nymph (nimf), and adult.

This Praying Mantis nymph looks like a tiny adult.

But it lacks the wings adults have.

It also can't produce young.

It needs to eat and grow bigger to become an adult.

Growing up in these three stages—egg, nymph, and adult—is called incomplete metamorphosis.

As a young insect grows bigger, it has to shed its skin, or molt.

Instead of having bones inside their bodies, insects have an exoskeleton.

It is like wearing a suit of armor.

This Cicada grew until its exoskeleton split open.

The insect crawled out, already wearing a new exoskeleton.

This new skin was soft at first, so the Cicada swelled even bigger.

That way, when the new exoskeleton hardened, it was roomy enough— for a while.

The number of times an insect molts depends on the kind of insect. Once the young insect becomes an adult, it stops growing and molting.

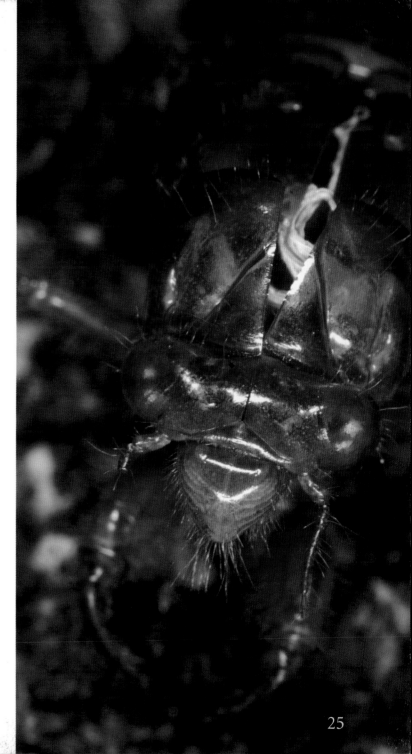

For an insect, growing up is all about becoming as big or as little as it was meant to be.

Some are little.

Others, like this male Hercules Beetle, are BIG.

That is how each different kind of insect has adapted to live in its own special part of the world.

For Hercules Beetle males, like Stag Beetle males, being big helps in fighting for mates. They use their big horns to battle with rivals.

Where in the World Do These Insects Live?

Check this map to see where the insects in this book were photographed. They may also be found in other parts of the world.

(Measurements show body length unless stated otherwise.)

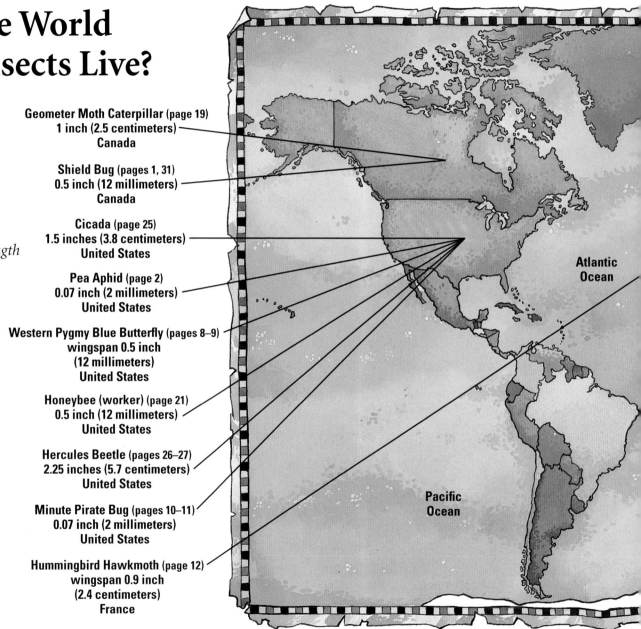

Geometer Moth Caterpillar (page 19)
1 inch (2.5 centimeters)
Canada

Shield Bug (pages 1, 31)
0.5 inch (12 millimeters)
Canada

Cicada (page 25)
1.5 inches (3.8 centimeters)
United States

Pea Aphid (page 2)
0.07 inch (2 millimeters)
United States

Western Pygmy Blue Butterfly (pages 8–9)
wingspan 0.5 inch
(12 millimeters)
United States

Honeybee (worker) (page 21)
0.5 inch (12 millimeters)
United States

Hercules Beetle (pages 26–27)
2.25 inches (5.7 centimeters)
United States

Minute Pirate Bug (pages 10–11)
0.07 inch (2 millimeters)
United States

Hummingbird Hawkmoth (page 12)
wingspan 0.9 inch
(2.4 centimeters)
France

Atlantic Ocean

Pacific Ocean

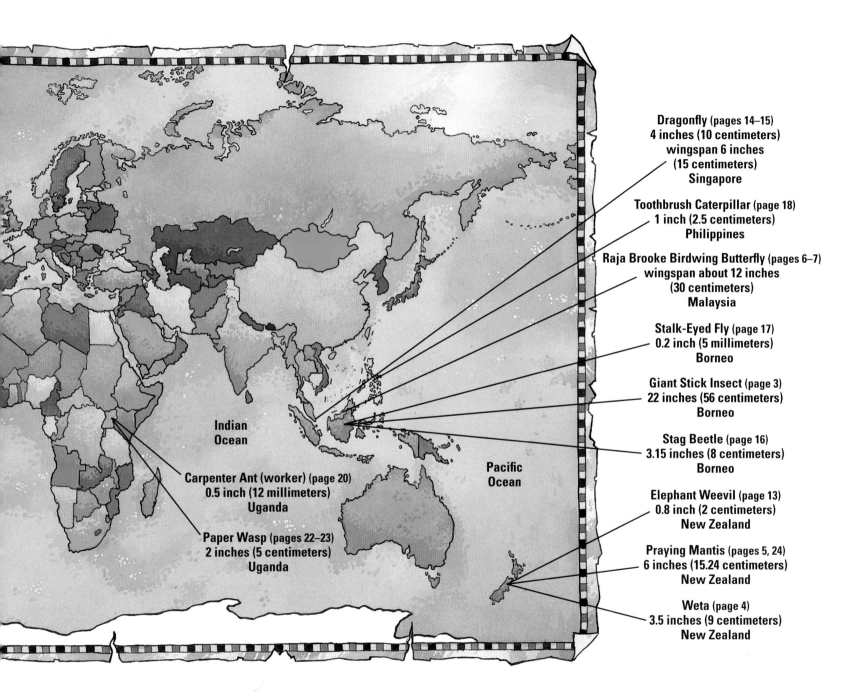

Dragonfly (pages 14–15)
4 inches (10 centimeters)
wingspan 6 inches
(15 centimeters)
Singapore

Toothbrush Caterpillar (page 18)
1 inch (2.5 centimeters)
Philippines

Raja Brooke Birdwing Butterfly (pages 6–7)
wingspan about 12 inches
(30 centimeters)
Malaysia

Stalk-Eyed Fly (page 17)
0.2 inch (5 millimeters)
Borneo

Giant Stick Insect (page 3)
22 inches (56 centimeters)
Borneo

Stag Beetle (page 16)
3.15 inches (8 centimeters)
Borneo

Elephant Weevil (page 13)
0.8 inch (2 centimeters)
New Zealand

Praying Mantis (pages 5, 24)
6 inches (15.24 centimeters)
New Zealand

Weta (page 4)
3.5 inches (9 centimeters)
New Zealand

Indian
Ocean

Pacific
Ocean

Carpenter Ant (worker) (page 20)
0.5 inch (12 millimeters)
Uganda

Paper Wasp (pages 22–23)
2 inches (5 centimeters)
Uganda

Insect Words You Learned

Adult [ah-DULT] the final stage of metamorphosis, in which the insect is fully developed and able to reproduce. *Adult* also means an insect in this stage.

Egg [eg] the female reproductive cell. *Egg* also means the fertilized egg that will produce a baby insect.

Exoskeleton [EKS-oh-SKEH-leh-ten] the armor-like body suit that gives an insect its shape and protects its soft inner body parts.

Larva [LAR-vuh] the second stage of complete metamorphosis, in which the young insect looks and behaves differently than the adult. *Larva* also means a young insect in this stage. Two or more are called larvae (LAR-vee).

Metamorphosis [MEH-tuh-MOR-feh-sis] the process that insects go through to become adults. Complete metamorphosis has four stages: egg, larva, pupa, adult. Incomplete metamorphosis has three stages: egg, nymph, adult.

Nectar [NEK-ter] sweet liquid produced by flowers that provides some insects, such as bees and butterflies, with food.

Nymph [nimf] the second stage of incomplete metamorphosis, in which the young looks and behaves like a small adult but is unable to reproduce. In insects that have wings as adults, the nymphs are wingless. *Nymph* also means a young insect in this stage.

Predator [PREH-deh-tor] an animal that catches other animals, its prey, to eat.

Prey [pray] an animal or animals that predators catch and eat.

Proboscis [pro-BAH-sis] a straw-like mouthpart that butterflies and moths use to sip nectar.

Pupa [PYU-puh] the third stage of complete metamorphosis, in which the young stops eating, goes into a protective covering, and changes into the adult form; also the name given to a young insect in this stage. Two or more are called pupae (PYU-pea).

For More Information

To find out more about insects, check out the following books and Web sites.

Books

Kalman, Bobbie, and John Crossingham. *Insect Homes*. The World of Insects Series. New York: Crabtree Publishing, 2006. Explore places some insects live, including homes they build for themselves.

Lovett, Sarah. *Extremely Weird Insects*. 2nd ed. Extremely Weird Series. Santa Fe, NM: John Muir Publications, 1996. Have fun investigating some of the world's most unusual insects.

Markle, Sandra. *Creepy, Crawly Baby Bugs*. New York: Walker, 1996. Find out how baby insects are born and behave as they grow up.

Web Sites*

Smithsonian Institution: Buginfo
www.si.edu/Encyclopedia_SI/nmnh/buginfo/start.htm
This site connects to lots of information about insects. Don't miss the link to "Fun Facts About Bugs."

*Active at time of publication

Bug Bios
www.insects.org
Find out more about insects and check out wonderful up-close photos.

The Field Museum: Butterfly Basics
www.fieldmuseum.org/exhibits/exhibit_sites/butterfly/basics.htm
This museum, based in Chicago, Illinois, shares the lives and behaviors of butterflies.

The insect on page 1 is a Shield Bug. It gets its name from its body shape. Shield Bugs are little insects, but they have a big defense. Special body parts between their first and second pairs of legs can give off a bad-smelling liquid. This defense makes most predators, such as birds, leave this insect alone. It's also why Shield Bugs are sometimes called stink bugs.

With love for Ruby Beckdahl and her brothers, Elijah and Noah
—S.M.

With love to my wife, Cynthia, and my parents, David and Dianna Pollard
—S.P.

Text copyright © 2009 by Sandra Markle
Photographs copyright © 2009 by Dr. Simon Pollard

Boyds Mills Press, Inc.
815 Church Street
Honesdale, Pennsylvania 18431
Printed in China

Library of Congress Cataloging-in-Publication Data

Markle, Sandra.
  Insects : biggest! littlest! / Sandra Markle ; photographs by Simon
Pollard. — 1st ed.
     p. cm.
  Includes bibliographical references.
  ISBN 978-1-59078-512-6 (hardcover : alk. paper)
  1. Insects—Juvenile literature. I. Pollard, Simon, ill. II. Title.

QL467.2.M3627 2009
595.7—dc22
                          2008033524

First edition
The text of this book is set in 18-point Minion.

10 9 8 7 6 5 4 3 2 1

Photo Credits: All photographs are by Dr. Simon Pollard except for pages 3 and 27 (Alex Wild), page 6 (Frans Lanting), page 9 (Dr. Peter Bryant), page 11 (Jack Dykinga–United States Department of Agriculture), and page 12 (Chris Mills).

Illustration Credit: Barry Mullins, page 3.

Acknowledgments: The author would especially like to thank Dr. Simon Pollard for sharing his expertise, enthusiasm, and exceptional photographs. As always, a thank-you to Skip Jeffery for his help and support throughout the creative process.

Note to Parents and Teachers: The books in the BIGGEST! LITTLEST! series encourage children to explore their world. Young readers are encouraged to wonder. They are guided to discover how animals depend on their special body features to succeed in their particular environments.

"Each plant or animal has different structures that serve different functions in growth, survival, and reproduction. An organism's patterns of behavior are related to the nature of that organism's environment, the availability of food, and the physical characteristics of the environment."
—National Science Education Standards as identified by the National Academy of Sciences